VISUAL EXPLORER GUIDE
GREECE

VISUAL EXPLORER GUIDE
GREECE

CLAUDIA MARTIN

amber
BOOKS

First published in 2021

Published by
Amber Books Ltd
United House
North Road
London
N7 9DP
United Kingdom
www.amberbooks.co.uk
Instagram: amberbooksltd
Facebook: amberbooks
Twitter: @amberbooks
Pinterest: amberbooksltd

Project Editor: Michael Spilling
Designer: Keren Harragan
Picture Research: Terry Forshaw

ISBN: 978-1-83886-099-8

Printed in China

Contents

Introduction   6

Athens and Attica   8

The Peloponnese   58

Central Greece   94

Northern Greece   116

Ionian Islands   140

Crete   160

Aegean Islands   180

Picture Credits   224

Introduction

A coastline of 13,600km (8,500 miles), as well as a topography notable for its rugged mountain ranges, have bestowed on Greece more than its fair share of natural wonders. The landscape ranges from agricultural plains to precipitous gorges, from shady olive groves to purple-flowered crocus fields. For millennia, Greece's inhabitants – both native and adventitious – have left their marks on this landscape.

The earliest great builders were the Minoans of Crete, who constructed the labyrinthine palace-centred city of Knossos from around 2,000 BCE. Later, the city-states of Classical Greece gave birth to some of the most refined structures ever built, from the temples of Athens to the treasures of Delphi. Over the centuries, the Romans added their monumental public buildings, the Byzantines their jewel-like monasteries, and the Venetians their castles. Perhaps most inventive of all are the many stories of Greece, from ancient myths to medieval folk tales, shedding light on landscape and buildings alike.

ABOVE:
Church of the Parigoritissa, Arta
OPPOSITE:
Leros, Dodecanese

Athens and Attica

Myth has it that Athens takes its name from the goddess of wisdom, Athena, yet it is more likely that she takes her name from the city. What is certain is that, by 900 BCE, Athens was a major centre in the region, thanks in part to the defensive stronghold of the Acropolis and easy access to the sea. In 508 BCE, Athenian leader Cleisthenes introduced democracy to the city-state. The decades that followed saw the city's Golden Age, during which the statesman Pericles embarked on a building programme on the Acropolis. In 338 BCE, the city lost its independence when Philip II of Macedon conquered all of Greece. Later, under the hellenophile Romans, Athens flourished, gaining vast temples, a gymnasium and library. After the fall of the Western Roman Empire, the city's fortunes also fell as it became no more than a provincial Byzantine trading town. In 1458, Athens was conquered by the Ottoman Empire, leading to centuries of decline. Following the Greek War of Independence, Athens was chosen as the Kingdom of Greece's new capital in 1834. A grand, modern city was designed, ushering in a new era.

OPPOSITE:

Mount Lycabettus, Athens

This hill is the subject of numerous myths. Some say that its name, possibly from the Greek *lycos* (wolf), was given in honour of the wolf pack that once roamed its wooded slopes. The hill itself is said to have been dropped by the goddess Athena as she was carrying limestone for the construction of the Acropolis.

Acropolis, Athens
The word *acropolis* comes from the Greek for 'high city'. This 150m (490ft) rocky outcrop, at the heart of modern Athens, was first inhabited in the 4th millennium BCE. The pillars of Hadrian's Library, built by Roman emperor Hadrian in 132 CE, can be seen in the foreground.

LEFT:
Caryatids,
Acropolis Museum
Five of the six caryatids
from the Acropolis's
Erechtheion are housed in
the Acropolis Museum.
The sixth, removed by
Lord Elgin, is on display
in the British Museum in
London. Caryatids are
named for the dancing
maidens of Karyai, in the
Peloponnese.

OVERLEAF:
Parthenon, Acropolis
This temple to the goddess
Athena, patron of Athens,
was built between 447 BCE
and 432 BCE. It replaced
an earlier temple that
was destroyed during
the Persian invasion of
480 BCE. The temple was
constructed in the Doric
style, characterized by
simple circular capitals at
the tops of its columns.

OPPOSITE:
Excavations, Acropolis Museum, Athens
The remains of a neighbourhood of ancient Athens,
dating from the 4th millennium BCE to the 12th century CE,
has been excavated beneath the Acropolis Museum itself.
Pictured here is a circular tower hall, dating from the 6th
century CE. Nearby are houses, baths and workshops.

OPPOSITE:

Parthenon, Acropolis

The Parthenon is an octostyle temple (with eight columns along front and back). Each column swells slightly halfway up, creating the illusion of being straight when viewed from a distance. At either end of the temple, the gable is topped by a triangular pediment once decorated with sculptures.

LEFT:

Erechtheion, Acropolis

Completed in 406 BCE, this temple was dedicated to Athena and Poseidon. The Porch of the Caryatids was built to hide the huge beam supporting the southwest corner. The (replica) caryatids on the left side of the porch balance on their right foot, while those on the right rest on their left foot.

17

OPPOSITE AND LEFT:

**Monastiraki Square,
Athens**

This central square is
named after the monastery
that once stood here, its
only remains the 10th-
century Church of the
Pantanassa (left). At the
back of the square is the
porticoed Tzistarakis
Mosque, built in 1759,
which has not functioned
as a mosque since
independence from the
Ottoman Empire.

The square is paved
with a mosaic of marble
(*see left*), stone and iron,
in a wave-like pattern
representing the historical
flow and diversity of the
peoples of this city. Just
off the square, and mixing
with its souvenir stalls,
is a fleamarket where
everything from old swords
to musical instruments can
be bought.

19

Feta

The first reference to a feta-like cheese was made in Homer's *Odyssey*, composed near the end of the 8th century BCE. Feta is a crumbly curd cheese made with sheep or goat's milk. It may be served simply sprinkled with oregano, on a salad or in traditional savoury pies.

Roasted Chestnuts and Corn

Stalls selling roasted chestnuts are a common sight in Athens and other Greek cities. Chestnuts have been a snack here for millennia, as evidenced by the 2nd-century writings of Galen of Pergamon, who mentioned their medicinal properties.

Grilled Lamb and Kokoretsi

Kokoretsi consists of lamb intestines wrapped around offal such as sweetbreads or kidney, then grilled. During Easter celebrations, *kokoretsi* is often eaten as an appetizer while a family waits for their spit-roasted lamb to be ready.

ABOVE:

Temple of Hephaestus, Ancient Agora of Athens
Built between 449 and 415 BCE, this temple dedicated to Hephaestus, god of fire and metalworking, stood in a neighbourhood of potteries and metalsmiths. It is in an exceptional state of preservation, since it remained in use after being converted into a Greek Orthodox church in the 7th century CE.

RIGHT:

Ancient Agora of Athens
The agora was the heart of classical Athens, a large gathering place surrounded by public buildings such as temples and stoas, which were covered walkways for the use of merchants and political or religious meetings. Later buildings can also be visited on the site, including the 11th-century Byzantine Church of the Holy Apostles.

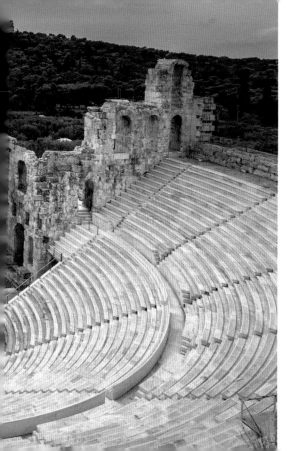

LEFT AND ABOVE:

Odeon of Herodes Atticus, Athens

Commissioned by the Greco-Roman senator Herodes
Atticus and completed in 167 CE, this odeon stands on the
southwest slope of the Acropolis. Like all odeons, it was
intended for musical concerts, so was originally covered by
a roof of cedar of Lebanon to benefit the acoustics.

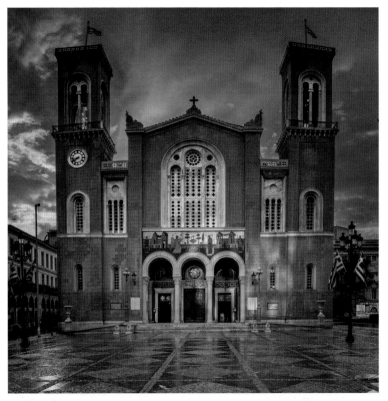

OPPOSITE AND LEFT:

**Metropolitan
Cathedral of Athens**
During the construction of
this cathedral, completed
in 1862, stone was taken
from 72 demolished
churches. Many of these
had not been destroyed by
the Ottomans, but were
seen as a useful source
of building materials.
Inside are the tombs of
two saints martyred under
Ottoman rule: Saint
Philothei (died 1589) and
Gregory V (died 1821).

OVERLEAF:

**View from Mount
Lycabettus, Athens**
Looking to the northwest
from Lycabettus, the green
tracts of Strefi Hill and
Field of Ares Park are
clear. The park honours
the heroes of the 1821
revolution – 21 of them
depicted in marble busts.

27

29

Athens Metro

The three-line Athens Metro network runs through 61 stations. Until 2000, there was only Line 1, in operation since 1869 and above ground apart from a tunnel section in central Athens. Both Lines 2 and 3 are largely underground, their inauguration greatly improving Athens' traffic congestion and air quality. The longest line at 25.6km (15.9 miles), Line 1 links the port of Piraeus with the wealthy suburb of Kifissia.

OPPOSITE:

Pláka, Athens
People relax in the Pláka neighbourhood. The district is built over a residential area of ancient Athens on the northern and eastern slopes of the Acropolis. During Ottoman rule, it was known as the Turkish quarter. Today, its streets are lined with whitewashed homes, museums, hotels, tavernas and cafés.

RIGHT:

Stoa ton Emboron, Athens
The 1950s 'Merchants' Arcade', near Syntagma Square, reopened in 2018 after a 20-year hiatus during which it fell into disrepair. The city council offered incentives to small businesses to rejuvenate the two-storey arcade, bringing back to life its retro neon signs.

ALL PHOTOGRAPHS:
Central Market, Athens
At the heart of Athens, on Athinas and surrounding streets, is Athens' central market, in operation since 1886. Stalls sell meat, fish, fruit and vegetables. Meat specialities include *soujouk* (beef sausage with cumin, garlic and red pepper) and *pastourma* (dehydrated beef or camel meat, prepared with herbs, garlic and paprika, then coated in cumin paste).

36

OPPOSITE:

Hellenic Parliament, Athens

The Greek parliament is a unicameral legislature comprising 300 members. It has been held in the Old Royal Palace, facing onto Syntagma Square, since 1934. The building itself was completed in 1843 for King Otto, the Bavarian prince who became the first king of modern Greece in 1832.

ABOVE:

Evzones at the Tomb of the Unknown Soldier, Athens

A ceremonial unit of soldiers guards the Tomb of the Unknown Soldier. Their uniforms are based on the clothing worn by *klephts*, the mountain insurgents who fought against the Ottomans. The kilt-like *foustanella* has 400 pleats to represent the liberation of Greece from nearly four centuries of Ottoman rule.

Zea Marina, Athens
Near the port of Piraeus is the superyacht marina of
Zea Bay. In ancient times, this was the city's biggest
harbour for military vessels. There were once docks
for nearly 200 *triremes*, fast warships with three rows
of oars. The ruined walls of the ancient harbour can
still be seen.

Laterna, Athens

The laterna, a variant of the barrel piano, was extremely popular in Greece in the late 19th and early 20th centuries. The barrel is turned by a crank. During the instrument's heyday, hundreds of laternas could be seen around Athens, but today only a handful remain.

BELOW AND OPPOSITE:

Pláka, Athens

Although most of Pláka is pedestrianized, strollers must beware the occasional speeding bike. The cobblestoned sidestreets become quieter as walkers ascend the slopes, entering the enclave of Anafiotika.

LEFT AND ABOVE:
Kalimarmaro Stadium, Athens

Also known as the Panathenaic Stadium, this is the world's only stadium built entirely of marble. It was first constructed in around 330 BCE for the Panathenaic Games, held every four years in ancient Athens. The stadium was later rebuilt in marble by the same Herodes Atticus who built the odeon on the Acropolis slopes. After being excavated in 1869, the site hosted the opening and closing ceremonies of the first modern Olympics in 1896. The stadium was once again an Olympic venue during the Athens Olympics of 2004.

LEFT AND OPPOSITE:
Academy of Athens
This national academy hosts numerous research centres, focussing on everything from Greek philosophy to climatology. The building was designed in Neoclassical style in 1859, by Danish architect Theophil Hansen. The pediment sculpture by Greek Neoclassicist Leonidas Drosis shows the birth of Athena. Hephaestus stands with hammer in hand after cracking Zeus' head to release the already armoured goddess. Drosis was also responsible for the figures of Athena and Apollo, holding a lyre, on the pillars that flank the imposing entrance.

Agistri, Saronic Islands

Just an hour's boat ride from Piraeus is the small,
pine-covered island of Agistri, in the Saronic Gulf.
Only around 1,000 people live here year round. On the
island's east coast is Chalikiada Beach, where nudists
camp in the summer months. It is only reachable by
foot, down a steep and slippery path.

Temple of Poseidon, Cape Sounion

This hexastyle temple (with a front portico supported
by six columns) was built from white marble in the
Doric style, in around 444–440 BCE. A previous temple
to Poseidon on the site was destroyed during Xerxes
I of Persia's invasion of Greece. Cape Sounion is the
southernmost tip of the Attic peninsula.

LEFT:

Mount Lycabettus Theatre

This amphitheatre, built in 1965 on the site of an old quarry, hosts summer performances of classical dramas as well as countless international acts, from Bob Dylan to Slipknot. It can seat up to 4,000 people.

ABOVE:

Plaster Masks, Pláka

During ancient theatre performances, actors wore masks of stiffened linen, painted to represent their character type. We know what they looked like from carvings and statues of actors made from more durable materials.

49

Aegina, Saronic Islands
Myth has it that this island draws its name from a nymph named Aegina, whose son, Aeacus, became the island's king. During ancient times, the island was a great sea power, rivalling even neighbouring Athens. Its location, between Attica and the Peloponnese, made its inhabitants rich from trade by at least 1700 BCE, when a hoard of Minoan gold was apparently buried in a tomb here. Only 40 minutes from Piraeus, Aegina is popular with weekending Athenians and even commuters.

Piraeus

The city of Piraeus was founded in the 5th century BCE, growing to become the largest port and harbour of ancient Greece. The port declined after the 3rd century BCE and was almost entirely deserted during Ottoman times. Piraeus regained importance after independence and the promotion of Athens to capital, growing once again into a bustling port and a municipality home to 160,000 people. The local football team, Olympiacos FC, has won more cups than any other Greek team.

53

ALL PHOTOGRAPHS:

Piraeus Port

Piraeus is Greece's biggest container port and the largest passenger port in Europe. Around 20 million passengers pass through every year, many of them boarding ferries to the Cyclades, Dodecanese and Crete. Its quays have an extraordinary total length of 2.8km (1.7 miles). For many travellers, Piraeus is no more than a waypoint, passed through at an awkward hour of the morning, after stumbling off Metro Line 1 from central Athens.

Spetses, Saronic Gulf
The island gets its name from the Italian *spezie*, meaning 'spices'. This dates from medieval times, when Venetians ruled the island and it served as a port on the spice route. Today, private cars are not allowed in the pretty town of Spetses, the main settlement on the island, although buzzing mopeds are plentiful.

RIGHT:
Hatzigiannis Mexis Mansion, Spetses
This 1798 mansion houses the Museum of Spetses, showcasing a local history that dates back to 2000 BCE. Hatzigiannis Mexis was a key local figure in the War of Independence. Spetses was one of the first Greek islands to join the revolution, on 3 April 1821.

The Peloponnese

From around 1600 BCE, the Peloponnese was at the centre of mainland Greece's first great civilization, Mycenae. Based around several palace-centred states, these traders dominated the eastern Mediterranean. The collapse of their civilization after around 500 years was followed by the so-called Dark Ages, before the first city-states, including Sparta and Argos, began to emerge from the 9th century BCE. According to the myths, the Peloponnese was first unified by the hero Pelops. During ancient times, Pelops was venerated at the Peloponnesian sanctuary of Olympia. Stories of his skill at chariot-racing may have led to the founding of the ancient Olympic Games.

The peninsula's wild interior is ruggedly mountainous, rising to its highest point, 2,404m (7,887ft), at Mount Taygetus. This isolating terrain led to the central region of Arcadia becoming a byword for an agricultural idyll. During the 19th and early 20th century, this same terrain led to economic isolation. Today, although the production of grapes, olives or oranges is still key, the region's immense wealth of ancient and medieval sites draw people from far and wide.

OPPOSITE:
Castle of Methoni, Methoni
In 1206 or 1207, Methoni was captured by the Venetians. They constructed a castle, large enough to be called a citadel, on a rocky promontory, separated from land by an an artificial moat. Methoni fell to the Ottomans in 1500.

Rio–Antirrio Bridge
Completed in 2004, this multi-span cable-stayed bridge crosses the Gulf of Corinth, linking the Peloponnese near Patras with Antirrio on the western mainland. Problems that had to be overcome by the bridge's engineers and architect, Berdj Mikaelian, included deep water over an unstable seabed, the expansion of the Gulf of Corinth due to tectonic activity, and the possibility of tsunamis. Beside the bridge is Rio Castle, built to protect the Corinthian Gulf by Ottoman Sultan Bayezid II in 1499. At 2,880m (9,450ft) long, with a suspended deck of 2,258m (7,408ft), the bridge has the world's longest fully suspended cable-stayed deck.

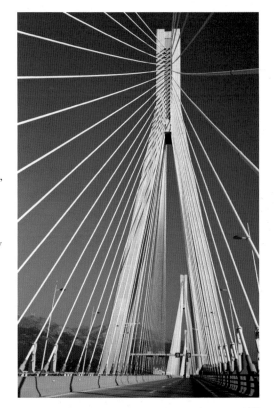

ABOVE AND OPPOSITE:

Larissa Castle, Argos

This rocky hilltop has been fortified for more than 2,000 years. The acropolis once formed part of the walls of the city of Argos, which was a major strategic and trading centre in the middle of the fertile plain of Argolis. There was a similar fortification on the nearby Aspis Hill, linked by a vast wall with gates to the city at each of the cardinal directions. The current fortress structure is partly Byzantine, dating from the 10th to 12th century. The fortress changed hands and was remodelled several times from the medieval period to 1822, with Crusader Franks, Venetians, Ottomans, Venetians again, and finally the Greeks taking control. Venetian polygonal bastions stand side by side with Ottoman round bastions.

LEFT:

St Peter's Church, Argos
One of the oldest settlements in Greece, the site of Argos is believed to have been continuously inhabited for 7,000 years. The Church of St Peter the Wondermaker, patron saint of the city, stands in the main square. St Peter, born in Constantinople in the late 9th century, became Bishop of Argos. It was said that the food he supplied for famine relief never ran out.

OPPOSITE:

Olympia
This religious sanctuary was the home of the ancient Olympic Games, held every four years from the 8th century BCE to the 4th century CE. It is in Olympia, at the Temple of Hera, that the Olympic flame is lit for each games.

OPPOSITE:

Gytheio

The 2nd-century CE Greek traveller and geographer Pausanias wrote in his *Description of Greece* that 'Heracles and Apollo, when they were reconciled after their fight for the possession of the tripod [of Delphi], worked together to found the city' of Gytheio. In fact, it is thought the Phoenicians were the first to settle here, collecting the plentiful murex sea snails to make purple dye.

LEFT:

Drying Octopus, Gytheio

Today, Gytheio is a busy fishing town, off the beaten track for most tourists, unless they have the time to explore the mountainous Mani Peninsula or are catching a ferry to Kythira. In the harbourfront tavernas, calamari and octopus, washed down with retsina, are staples.

OVERLEAF:

Theatre of Epidaurus

Built on the west side of Mount Kinortio, this 4th-century BCE theatre was praised in antiquity for its elegant design and excellent acoustics and stage views. The auditorium is divided into upper and lower parts by a corridor to allow the passage of spectators. The lower part is in 12 wedges, while the upper is in 22. Unlike most Greek theatres, it was not modified by the Romans.

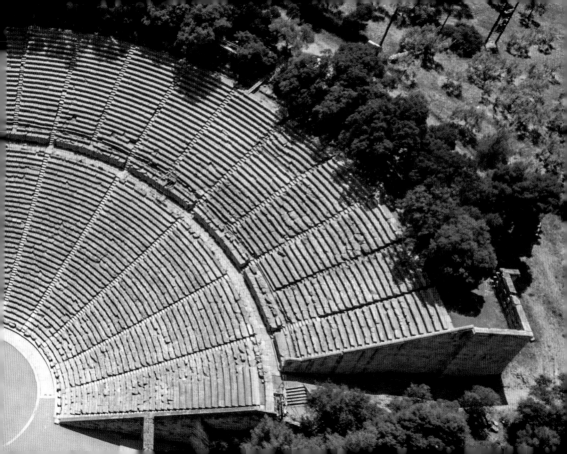

Diros Caves, Areopoli

These partially flooded caves were rediscovered in 1895, since when around 14km (9 miles) of passages have been explored. The caves were inhabited from Neolithic times until 4 BCE, when they were abandoned due to an earthquake. Parts of the cave system were also used for burials and rituals. In 2014, the remains of an embracing couple, dated to around 3,800 BCE, were found inside.

Pylos

Once an important Mycenaean kingdom, Pylos has also been known as Port-de-Jonc, during Frankish rule, and Navarino, under the Venetians. Today, this small, pretty town, facing onto an immense bay of the Ionian Sea, draws visitors to its unspoiled beaches. Koukos (The Cuckoo) serves traditional grills and oven bakes such as moussaka.

St Andrew's Cathedral, Patras
The largest church in Greece, this Greek Orthodox basilica was begun in 1908 but not inaugurated until 1974. It is an eclectic design, incorporating Byzantine, Russian and Mughal influences. The central cupola is 46m (150ft) tall, crowned with a cross representing Christ, while 12 smaller crosses symbolize the Apostles.

Interior of St Andrew's Cathedral
Relics of St Andrew the Apostle are stored in a shrine inside the church. The relics consist of his little finger, part of his skull and a portion of the diagonal cross on which he is believed to have been martyred in Patras, after travelling to Greece to preach the Gospel.

ALL PHOTOGRAPHS:

Corinth Canal

The 6.4-km (4-mile) Corinth Canal effectively turned the Peloponnesian peninsula into an island. The canal links the Saronic Gulf of the Aegean Sea with the Gulf of Corinth of the Ionian Sea. The idea of a canal was first proposed, but not acted on, by Periander, ruler of Corinth in the 7th century BCE. In the event, construction started in 1881 and, thanks to numerous engineering difficulties, lasted until 1893. Due to the canal's width of 21.4m (70ft), traffic is limited. Larger ships must be towed through and a one-way system is in operation.

Ancient Corinth
From the 8th century BCE, Corinth grew to be one of the most important Greek city-states. By the start of the 4th century BCE, its population was around 90,000. It was at this time that the city's architects developed the Corinthian style, the most ornate of the three main classical Greek forms, characterized by slender fluted columns and elaborate capitals.

Pirene Fountain, Ancient Corinth
The Pirene spring was said to be the favoured watering hole of the winged horse Pegasus. This fountain had taken something close to its current structure by the 2nd century BCE: six cave-like chambers provide access to three basins supplied with spring water by channels under the forum.

Temple of Apollo, Ancient Corinth
Only seven columns remain of the original 38 of this mid-6th century BCE Doric temple. The structure contained two rooms, the smaller probably acting as a treasury, although some scholars believe it was dedicated to the cult of Artemis, Apollo's sister. Built on high ground, the temple would have been visible across Corinth.

Plain of Mantineia, near Tripoli

This valley, patchworked by vineyards, pastures, and potato and wheat farms, lies in the modern regional unit of Arcadia. A few hundred people here still speak Tsakonian, which has its roots in ancient Doric Greek but is not intelligible to modern Greek speakers. Myth tells us that the region took its name from the hunter Arcas, who taught people how to weave and bake.

During the Renaissance, the region's mountainous landscape and sparse population of shepherds and farmers caused 'arcadia' to become a byword for an idyllic, unspoiled wilderness. An arcadia was a lost Eden, where people maintained a simple way of life.

OPPOSITE:

Prodromou Monastery, Lousios Gorge

This 16th-century monastery is dedicated to St John the Baptist. It clings to the cliff of the deep, 15-km (9-mile) Lousios Gorge, near Stemnitsa. The Lousios Gorge is known as 'the Mount Athos of the Peloponnese', due to the many monasteries that perch in its shelter.

ABOVE:

Stemnitsa, Lousios Gorge

The village of Stemnitsa huddles at an elevation of 1,050m (3,450ft), hemmed in by the Mainalo Mountains. The name of the village comes from the Slavic for 'woodland', signalling the Slavic roots of many of the villagers, whose families arrived in the 7th and 8th centuries.

Church of Sts Theodores, Mystras

The fortified city of Mystras was built
by the Byzantines from the 13th century.
It became the centre of Byzantine power
in southern Greece with monasteries,
churches, palaces, public squares and
homes. After 1460, Mystras was occupied
by the Turks and Venetians, before being
abandoned and left to fall into ruins by
its inhabitants, who moved down the
hill to modern Sparta, from 1834. The
octagonal-plan Church of Sts Theodores
dates from 1290–95.

Interior of Church of St Nicholas, Mystras

The 16th-century Church of St Nicholas
has wall paintings depicting scenes from
the life of the saint, in comic book form.
St Nicholas (c. 270–342) was the bishop
of the Greek city of Myra, in modern-day
Turkey. His habit of secret gift-giving gave
rise to the legend of Santa Claus.

FAR LEFT:
**Monastery of
St Nicholas of Sintza,
near Leonidio**
Built inside a cave on an
almost sheer cliff face
is this hard-to-reach
monastery, established in
the 13th century. Most
of the current buildings
date from the 18th
century, as does the icon
of the saint himself.
'Sintza' means fig tree in
the Tsakonian dialect.

LEFT:
**Easter Celebrations,
Leonidio**
Every Easter, following
the announcement of
Christ's resurrection,
hundreds of small hot-air
balloons are released into
the sky over Leonidio. The
paper balloons trail rags
soaked in petrol, which
are set alight.

Farmer's Market, Kalamata

Although most famous for its dark purple olives, the fertile soil and mild climate of the Kalamata region also produce grapes, figs, almonds, oranges and citrons. Local wine-producing grape varieties include the white Moschofilero, with a pink skin and spicy flavour, and the red, fruity Agiorgitiko.

OPPOSITE LEFT:

Fish Market, Kalamata

The local catch in Kalamata, the chief port of the Messenia region, includes grouper, sea bream and tuna. Fish restaurants line the seafront, so diners can watch their lunch straight from the boat to their plate.

OPPOSITE RIGHT:

Artos Bread, Proastio

Loaves of artos bread are shared in the village square to celebrate a saint's day. The leavened bread is usually baked at home, then brought to the church to be blessed by the priest.

Treasury of Atreus, Mycenae

From 1600 to 1100 BCE, Mycenae was a major power, dominating southern Greece, Crete and the Cyclades. Several beehive tombs were built here, by digging the internal chamber like a well, walling it with rings of stones, then covering it with earth. The Treasury of Atreus (c. 1250 BCE) held the remains of an unknown monarch.

BELOW:

Lion Gate, Mycenae

This gateway was the main entrance to the walled city, erected in around 1250 BCE. Above its lintel is a relief sculpture of two lions, their heads missing. The gateway is 3.1m (10ft) wide and 2.95m (10ft) high. The lion gate was still visible in the 2nd century CE, when it was described by the travel writer Pausanias.

Tolo Beach

The bay of Tolo was first written about by Homer in the *Iliad*. Since the middle of the 20th century, Tolo has become a small resort for Greek tourists and a few from further afield. The 1-km (0.6-mile) beach is backed by dunes, as well as restaurants, bars and hotels. With fine sand and gently sloping shallows, the spot is popular with young families.

LEFT:

Monemvasia

This fortified town, on a flat-topped rocky islet, is linked to the mainland by a 200-m (650-ft) modern causeway. Monemvasia was founded in the 6th century by refugees from the mainland during the Avaro-Slavic invasions. From the 10th century, it became an important trading centre.

ABOVE:

Church of St Sophia, Monemvasia

Standing at Monemvasia's highest point, with a vertiginous view over the cliff edge, is this 13th-century church. It was originally commissioned by Byzantine emperor Andronicus II, but has Venetian additions from its days as a convent.

Central Greece

Central Greece is at the heart of Greece both geographically and culturally. In ancient times, the sanctuary of Delphi, on the slopes of Mount Parnassus, was home to an all-powerful female oracle. The Greeks considered Delphi to be both the physical centre of the world and central to decision-making. Also in this region were key city-states such as Thebes, a major rival to ancient Athens. Many mythological events took place in the region, from the launch of Jason's *Argo* to the Battle of the Titans between the older generation of gods, the Titans, and the young Olympians, on the Plain of Thessaly. Despite its largely mountainous topography, this region is one of Greece's most populated. It boasts some of Greece's largest, liveliest cities, including Larissa, Volos, Trikala, Chalcis and Lamia. For visitors, this region offers Greece in microcosm, from its photogenic ancient sites to its rock-perched Byzantine monasteries hoarding jewel-like icons. Its landscapes range from the agricultural Plain of Thessaly to the snow-capped mountains of Phocis, from popular resorts on Euboea to untouched beaches on the Pelion Peninsula.

OPPOSITE:
Proussos Monastery, Karpenisi
Reached by a narrow, terrifying road edged by a cliff on one side and a gorge on the other, this monastery clings to the cliff face, its main church housed in a cave. The monastery's silver-rich icon of the Virgin is believed to be miraculous, drawing the faithful from around Greece and beyond.

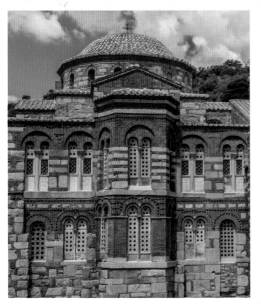

ABOVE:

Hosios Loukas Monastery

This Byzantine monastery on the slopes of Mount
Helicon was founded in the 10th century by St Luke
of Steiris. The monastery's fine architecture is in part
thanks to the wealth brought by the saint's relics, which
were said to exude a balm that cured the sick.

ABOVE AND OPPOSITE:

Interior of the Katholikon, Hosios Loukas Monastery

This domed, octagonal church dates from the early
11th century. Glittering on its many curving surfaces
are fine examples of Middle Byzantine mosaics,
featuring the Virgin and Child, angels and many heavy-
eyed, bearded saints.

Lagoon of Missolonghi

The extensive lagoons and wetlands close to the port of Missolonghi, on the Gulf of Patras, are vital ecosystems for fish, amphibians, birds and plants. Traditional flat-bottomed fishing boats, called *gaites*, are still used for navigating the shallow waters. Some are even today powered by oars, but most have an outboard motor.

LEFT AND ABOVE:

Vlach Wedding, Thebes

Every year during Carnival, the Vlach Wedding ritual takes places in Thebes. It is a mix of ancient Dionysian rites and traditions brought by the Vlachs, a Balkan people who speak a language descended from Latin. On the Sunday, around seven teams, numbering at least 30 people each, set off from the homes of their captains, all dressed in traditional Vlach costumes and holding shepherds' crooks. Making as much noise as possible, they converge on the main square for dancing. The following day, Clean Monday – the beginning of Orthodox Lent – a comic 'wedding' is acted out by the 'bride', 'groom' and bystanders, all in the Vlach language. Finally, the 'groom' pretends to die and is resurrected to great rejoicing.

LEFT:
Tower of Mytikas, Euboea

One of a pair of 15th-century Venetian forts, built on a low hill on the island of Euboea, this tower may once have had clock faces on its sides, making it one of the earliest clock towers in Greece. The towers were probably built to guard the water supply of nearby Chalcis, as the River Lilandas flows nearby. They also offered a refuge to local people during bandit attacks.

OPPOSITE:
Krya Spings, Livadeia

This pretty oasis is in the heart of Livadeia, today a modest town but in ancient times a famed spot due to the presence of the oracle of Trophonius. Trophonius was a god or mythological hero, or something in between. Whoever wanted to consult the oracle would live in a house in Livadeia for a set number of days, bathing in the waters of this river and sacrificing to the gods. Finally, they would descend into a nearby cave to hear the words of the oracle, an experience that seemingly frightened most out of their wits.

OPPOSITE:

General store, Chalcis, Euboea

The largest town on the island of Eubeoa, Chalcis was first mentioned in Homer's *Iliad*, described as being near the gathering point for ships heading to the Trojan War. Euboea is 180km (110 miles) long, but only 6km (3.7 miles) wide at its narrowest point.

LEFT:

Limni, Euboea

The port of Limni is the site of the annual 14.5km (9 mile) Skyllias swimming marathon to Theologos, on the mainland. It is named after the Greek hero Scyllis who, in 480 BCE, was taken prisoner on a Persian ship. After hearing of an impending attack on the Greek navy, Scyllis escaped and cut all the Persian ships loose.

OPPOSITE:

Tholos, Delphi

From around the 8th century BCE to the 4th century CE, the high priestess of Delphi's Temple of Apollo, known as the Pythia, was an oracle of such power that no important decision could be taken without consulting her. The most photographed spot in Delphi's large religious complex is undoubtedly the circular Tholos, at the sanctuary of Athena Pronoia ('Athena of Forethought'), which was constructed between 380 and 360 BCE.

ABOVE:

East Frieze from Siphnian Treasury, Delphi

Erected around 525 BCE, this treasury housed offerings to Apollo from the city-state of Siphnos, in the Cyclades. Its lavish sculptures can be seen in the Delphi Archeological Museum. The East Frieze shows an assembly of the gods, who appear to be raising their arms in argument as they take sides over the Trojan War.

LEFT:

Replica of the *Argo*, Volos

The *Argo* was the ship on which the mythical hero Jason and the Argonauts sailed from Iolcus, which stood on the site of modern Volos. Ancient authors imagined that the *Argo* was shaped like a Greek galley warship.

OPPOSITE:

Agia Kyriaki, Pelion Peninsula

The Pelion Peninsula curls like a finger about to flick the islands of Skiathos and Skopelos in the Aegean Sea to the east. Near the peninsula's southwestern tip is the small fishing village of Agia Kyriaki, where a few yachts moor during the summer months, but otherwise the pace of life is much as it has been for centuries.

Volos Railway Station

The city of Volos grew rapidly after Thessaly's incorporation into the Kingdom of Greece in 1881. Many of the city's grand, neoclassical buildings date from this time. The 1884 railway station was designed by Italian Evaristo de Chirico.

Lake Plastiras

This reservoir is named after the Greek prime minister Nikolaos Plastiras (1883–1953), who first suggested the project. A 1960 concrete arch dam prevents flooding of the River Tavropos while providing hydroelectric power and water to the nearby city of Karditsa.

Varlaam Monastery, Meteora
In the northwestern Plain of Thessaly is a region where
huge pillars of sandstone and conglomerate have been
eroded by weathering along vertical faults. From the
14th century, devoted monks built monasteries on these
rocks to avoid Ottoman attacks. Access was only by
ladder or winch. Of the original 24 monasteries, six
remain today. Varlaam Monastery was founded in the
mid-14th century by the exercitant Hosios Varlaam.
All alone, he built three churches, a cell for himself and
a water tank. The Katholikon (right) was built in the
mid-16th century and lavishly decorated with frescoes
and icons.

OPPOSITE LEFT:
Roussanou Monastery, Meteora
This monastery takes its name from that of the first
hermit who settled on the rock. Its main church was
built in the 16th century. Today, it is a convent with
around a dozen nuns still in residence.

OPPOSITE RIGHT:
Interior of Holy Trinity Monastery, Meteora
Filling a wall niche, this fresco of the Virgin and Child
is in Holy Trinity, perched on a 400m (1,310ft) rock.
It is the most difficult monastery to reach, via 140 steps.

Northern Greece

This eclectic region is sometimes called the New Lands since it covers the regions of Epirus, Macedonia and Thrace, which did not join the Kingdom of Greece until after the Balkan Wars of 1912–13. Thrace was the last region to join, when it was ceded by Bulgaria in 1919. Yet there is nothing new about these regions. It was a king of Macedon, Philip II (382–336 BCE), who in 337 BCE conquered and politically consolidated most of Greece. While Greece had previously been united by a shared culture, this was the first time it had edged towards being a single entity – something that was not to happen until the 20th century. Yet the culture, food, monasteries, mosques and towns of northern Greece bear witness to the fact that the region's long history has been formed not only by its own people but by those from farther afield, including Romans, Byzantines, Slavs and Turks. The landscape here is also among the most varied in Greece, from the wooded plains of Thrace to the Pindus Mountains and the canyon of Vikos Gorge.

OPPOSITE:
Florina
The motto of the city of Florina, 13km (8 miles) south of the border with the Republic of North Macedonia, is 'Where Greece begins'. Thanks in part to its elevation at 687m (2,254ft), Florina is one of the coldest towns in Greece. Thick fog and heavy snowfalls are common during winter, when the temperature has been known to drop to -29°C (-20°F).

Mount Olympus

With a circumference of 150km (93 miles), Mount Olympus has 52 peaks and numerous gorges. The tallest peak, Mytikas, has an elevation of 2,917m (9,570ft), making it the highest point in Greece. In the religion of ancient Greece, the 12 main Greek gods lived on Mount Olympus. Wherever Greek people lived, they tended to designate the highest point as Mount Olympus. However, by around the 5th century BCE, this peak came to be seen as the Pan-Hellenic Olympus.

St Panteleimon Monastery, Mount Athos
The Mount Athos peninsula, dominated by the mountain of the same name, is home to 20 Eastern Orthodox monasteries. Around 2,000 monks from Greece and other Eastern Orthodox countries, such as Bulgaria, Georgia, Moldova, Romania, Russia and Serbia, live on this isolated peninsula.

Saffron Field, Near Kozani
The Kozani region, and in particular the town of Krokos, is renowned for its high-quality saffron production. The Greek red saffron grown here has a bright colour and strong flavour. The name of the crocus genus comes from the Greek word *krokos*, meaning 'saffron', which itself derives from Sanskrit.

ALL PHOTOGRAPHS THIS PAGE:

Cuisine of Thessaloniki

Thessaloniki's old port-side district of Ladadika (*near right*) is renowned for its tavernas, cafés and bars, many of them located in the old olive oil shops that once thronged the area. This is the place to try local delicacies, such as *koulouri* (*bottom right*), a circular bread encrusted with sesame seeds and found across the former Ottoman Empire. The Ottoman Empire was also a cradle of coffee culture. However, it was not until 1957 that the popular café frappé was accidentally invented by a Nescafe representative in Thessaloniki. On sale in Thessaloniki's many markets is *graviera* (*top right*), Greece's second most popular cheese, after feta.

Thessaloniki and the Thermaic Gulf

The Thermaic Gulf, in the northwestern corner of the Aegean Sea, is named after the ancient city of Therma, which stood close to modern Thessaloniki. Therma, founded in the late 7th century BCE, was itself named after the word for 'fever', thanks to its location in a mosquito-infested swamp.

OPPOSITE:

Hagia Sophia, Thessaloniki

This Byzantine Greek-cross basilica was erected in the 8th century, inspired by the Hagia Sophia of Constantinople. In 1430, when Thessaloniki was taken by the Ottomans, it was converted into a mosque, then in 1912 became a church again when the city was liberated from Ottoman rule.

RIGHT:

Rotunda, Thessaloniki

This monumental circular structure, once with an oculus (opening) in the centre of its roof, was built for Roman Emperor Galerius in 306 CE. It has served as a Roman temple, Christian church and Ottoman mosque, from which period it retains a minaret.

RIGHT:

Parga

Known as the 'Bride of Epirus', the amphitheatre-shaped town of Parga faces onto the Ionian Sea. In summer, visitors throng Parga's colourfully painted restaurants and cafés thanks to its sandy beaches and turquoise sea, dotted with picture-perfect islets.

OPPOSITE:

Lake Kerkini

A reservoir created by the damming of the River Struma, Kerkini is a vitally important hydrobiosphere, close to the border with Bulgaria. Among the 227 species of birds found here is the Dalmatian pelican (pictured), the largest pelican, with a wingspan of up to 3.5m (11.5ft).

Bridge of Arta

There has been a bridge across the River Arachthos here, in Epirus, since the days of Roman rule. It has been rebuilt many times since, with the current incarnation probably dating from the early 17th century. The 'Bridge of Arta' folk ballad, possibly dating from Byzantine times, tells the story of the bridge's interminable, existentially challenging construction: 'All day they were building it, and in the night it would collapse.' This led to a number of popular proverbs.

Aristotelous Square, Thessaloniki
The main square of Greece's second largest city is appropriately monumental. It was designed by Frenchman Ernest Hébrard in 1918, taking inspiration from Byzantine architecture, but not actually constructed until the 1950s.

LEFT:
Zongolopoulos Umbrellas, Thessaloniki
George Zongolopoulos (1903–2004) was a major Greek sculptor and architect who constantly challenged and experimented. His works, including this iconic seafront display, frequently featured umbrellas.

ABOVE:
Pozar Thermal Baths
In a gorge at the foot of Mount Kaimaktsalan are the
Pozar thermal springs, where the Agios Nikolaos River,
also known as Thermopotamos ('hot river' in ancient
Greek) reaches 37°C (98.6°F). Pozar means 'fire' in
Slavic, a dialect spoken by the Macedonian people of
this region.

OPPOSITE:
Vikos Gorge
In the Pindus Mountains, the 20km (12 mile) Vikos
Gorge is the world's deepest gorge relative to its width.
It reaches 490m (1,600ft) deep, while its width ranges
from 400m (1,300ft) to just a few metres. This chasm
was the work of the Voidomatis River. Hikers may spot
chamois at higher elevations.

OPPOSITE:

Ouranoupoli

The modern village of Ouranoupoli is on the site of
ancient Uranopolis, a city said to have been founded
by Alexarchus of Macedon in the 3rd century BCE. The
tower overlooking the beach was built in the early 14th
century by monks from a nearby monastery, to watch
over the sea for impending attacks. The upper two floors
were rebuilt by the Ottomans.

ABOVE:

Near Pyrgos Sani

Even in the popular tourist region of Chalkidiki, close
to the developed resort of Pyrgos Sani, agricultural life
continues. As for centuries, green olives, olive oil, honey
and wine are major products. In the 1950s, tourism
started to develop here, mainly catering to visitors
from nearby Thessaloniki. By the 1970s, international
tourism was booming.

OPPOSITE:

Elatochori, Pieirian Mountains

With 12km (7.5 miles) of slopes at heights of between 1,400m and 1,900m (4,600–6,200ft), the village of Elatochori is growing in popularity as a winter sports resort. The rest of the year, it offers respite from the overheated coast in its quiet woods perfect for collecting chestnuts and walnuts.

BELOW:

Church of the Parigoritissa, Arta

This Byzantine church was commissioned in around 1290 by the Despot of Epirus, Nikephoros I Komnenos Doukas. The Despotate of Epirus was a breakaway state from the Byzantine Empire. The almost-square church has three-storeys, a central dome, and four smaller domes on its flat roof.

OPPOSITE:
St Nicholas Monastery, Porto Lagos

A satellite monastery of Vatopedi at Mount Athos, St Nicholas is on a small island in Lake Vistonida. During Ottoman times, the daughter of the local *bey* was cured by a monk from Vatopedi, resulting in the *bey* donating land for a new monastery.

LEFT:
Xanthi

In the foothills of the Rhodope Mountains, Xanthi's red-roofed old town is a treasure trove of Byzantine churches, Ottoman mosques and Neoclassical merchants' mansions. The town may be named after one of the mythological Amazons, warrior women who were said to once rule this northeastern region.

139

Ionian Islands

The Ionian Islands are sometimes known as the Heptanese ('Seven Islands') for the seven largest: Corfu, Paxos, Lefkada, Ithaca, Cephalonia, Zakynthos and Kythira. The first six lie in the Ionian Sea, but Kythira is in the Aegean, off the south coast of the Peloponnese. However, the islands share a cultural identity, due to their long Venetian rule, beginning with the capture of Kythira in the mid-14th century and ending in the late 18th century. This was followed by periods of French and British rule,

before joining Greece in 1864. This multinational history is evidenced by the islands' many names: 'Corfu', for example, is the Italian name for the Greek 'Kerkyra'. These islands' ethereal beauty is reflected by the many myths that surround them. Kythira was said to have been the birthplace of Aphrodite, goddess of love. There are arguments for several of the Ionian Islands being the island of Ithaca described in Homer's *Odyssey*, although modern Ithaca itself is the most likely. Ithaca was the home of the legendary king Odysseus.

OPPOSITE:
Cape Drastis, Corfu
At Corfu's northwestern point is this wind- and wave-sculpted cape, said to resemble a mother turtle with her babies swimming alongside. It is not possible to descend the steep cliffs from the narrow road above, but the small clay and sand beaches can be reached by boat in good weather.

Antisamos Beach, Cephalonia
This lovely pebble beach is backed by scrub- and Greek fir-clad hills. The beach grows popular at the height of summer, in part thanks to the international fame gained by its use as a location in the 2001 film *Captain Corelli's Mandolin*, starring Nicolas Cage and Penélope Cruz.

OPPOSITE:
Achilleion Palace, Corfu

Corfu was Empress Elisabeth of Austria's favourite holiday destination. This palace was built for her in 1890, while she was grieving for the apparent suicide of her only son, Rudolf. The residence was styled as a romantic ancient palace, with the hero Achilles a central theme, as suggested by its name.

ABOVE:
Grand Staircase, Achilleion Palace

The vast palace was designed by Italian architect Raffaele Caritto in a broadly Pompeiian style. Elisabeth wrote of her plans: 'I want a palace with pillared colonnades and hanging gardens.' For finishing touches, the great German sculptor Ernst Herter created works inspired by Greek mythology.

Kioni, Ithaca

The unspoilt village of Kioni is on the northeast coast of the island of Ithaca, which is almost divided in half by the narrow Isthmus of Aetos. This hilly, rugged island has few beaches, drawing travellers with the prettiness of its villages, its ancient ruins and the breathtaking views along its many hikes.

Lakka, Paxos

The almost circular harbour of the fishing village of Paxos is sheltered from the open sea by two headlands. Small beaches are dotted around the bay, squeezed between the turquoise sea and the encroaching olive groves and cypress trees. In summer, the water is busy with yachts, windsurfers and swimmers.

ALL PHOTOGRAPHS:

Angelokastro, Corfu
Built in the 13th century,
this Byzantine castle
perches on a rocky clifftop
300m (1,000ft) above the
sea. Over the centuries,
Angelokastro played a
decisive role in warding
off three Ottoman sieges,
in 1537, 1571 and 1716.
Under the Venetians from
1387 to the end of the 16th
century, Angelokastro
was the official capital of
Corfu and the seat of the
governor of the Ionian
Islands and commander
of the Venetian fleet.

LEFT:

Kumquat Liqueur and Sweets, Corfu

Kumquat is a citrus tree that bears oval, orange fruits with a sweet and acidic taste. Native to Asia, kumquats were introduced to Corfu in the 19th century by the English botanist Sydney Merlin. Today the fruit is grown locally and used to make liqueurs and sweets.

OPPOSITE:

St Spyridon Church, Corfu Town

The bell tower of the 16th-century church is the tallest in the Ionian Islands. It houses the relics of St Spyridon (c. 270–348), patron saint of the island. In 1453, the relics were brought to the island by a monk from Constantinople, when that city fell to the Ottomans.

Prickly Pears

Prickly pears, known in the Ionian Islands as *frangosyka*, meaning 'Frankish figs', were possibly introduced during late Venetian times. These cacti were often planted around fortifications to offer an extra level of impenetrability. When carefully peeled, the fruits may be eaten raw or used to make a honey syrup.

Figs

Figs have been widely grown here since ancient times. The fruit is eaten fresh or dried, turned into preserves or spoon sweets, or baked into spiced, liqueur-rich cakes known as *sykomaitha*.

Olives

There are somewhere between two and four million olive trees on the island of Corfu alone. The climate is ideal here for olive production, with mild winters and long, hot summers. Corfu is known for its high-quality virgin olive oil, as well as its oils enriched with aromas of herbs.

Blue Caves, Zakynthos

At Zakynthos's northernmost point, below the lighthouse at Cape Skinari, the waves have sculpted arches and caves into the cliffs. Glittering reflections between turquoise water and pale limestone walls seem to turn everything and everyone that enters the water an otherworldly blue.

ABOVE:
Navagio Beach, Zakynthos

Backed by sheer cliffs, Navagio (meaning 'shipwreck') Beach is accessible only by boat. Before 1980, the beach was known as Agios Georgios. Then a freighter, the MV *Panagiotis*, ran aground here. The beach found fame in the hugely popular 2016 South Korean drama *Descendants of the Sun*.

OPPOSITE:
Nidri Waterfalls, Lefkada
On a summer's day, the cooling waterfalls near the town of Nidri are a popular destination for swimming. Connected to the mainland by a causeway, Lefkada is one of the few islands that is reachable by car.

ABOVE:
Kavalikefta Beach, Lefkada
On Lefkada's quieter west coast, Kavalikefta is known for its giant rocks, making sunbathers feel as if they are mere ants among pebbles. The beach is reached down a nerve-rackingly narrow switchbacking road.

Church, Old Perithia, Corfu

The mountain village of Perithia was abandoned in the 1960s, becoming a ghost town as its inhabitants moved to the coast to find work, largely in the tourist industry. In its heyday, Perithia was home to 1,200 people and one of the wealthiest settlements on the island, surrounded by vineyards, oak trees and pastures. Since 2010, when one of the merchant's houses was renovated and opened as a bed-and-breakfast, the village has begun to prick into life once more, although it remains uniquely suspended in time.

Crete

Stone tools found in southern Crete suggest that the largest of the Greek Islands may have been inhabited for as long as 130,000 years. Certainly, from around 7000 BCE, Crete boasted numerous Neolithic settlements. From 2700 BCE to 1100 BCE, Crete was home to Europe's first advanced civilization: the Minoans. The Minoans developed a writing system, constructed monumental architecture and created beautiful artworks. The centre of their complex world was the city of Knossos, in northern Crete.

The Minoans did not call themselves by this name. The term refers to the mythical King Minos of Crete, associated in Greek mythology with the labyrinth, lair of the Minotaur – a ferocious creature that was part man, part bull.

The first archeologist of Knossos, Arthur Evans, linked the site with Minos because of the palace's maze-like layout and bull iconography. Minos was the son of Zeus, king of the gods, who was himself said to have been born in a cave on the island.

OPPOSITE:
Agios Nikolaos
In the Bay of Mirabello, Agios Nikolaos is known for its chic, low-key nightlife. A narrow channel separates the town's harbour from the circular Lake Voulismeni, its shore lined with lounge-bars and tavernas. The town's patron saint, St Nicholas, is the patron saint of fishermen.

LEFT:

St Minas Cathedral, Heraklion

This large cruciform cathedral was built between 1862 and 1895. The cathedral is dedicated to St Minas (285–309 CE), an Egyptian soldier in the Roman army who was martyred because he refused to recant his Christian faith.

OPPOSITE:

Heraklion Harbour

Crete's largest city still boasts many of the fortifications that protected it during Venetian rule. In the 16th and 17th centuries this was one of the most well-fortified towns in the Mediterranean. However, after one of the longest sieges in history, lasting from 1648 to 1669, the city fell to the Ottomans.

North Entrance, Knossos
From around 2000 BCE,
the palace was the centre
of Minoan civilization.
The North Entrance was
partially reconstructed
by Arthur Evans, the
English archeologist who
unearthed the palace
at the turn of the 20th
century. The monumental
gateway's bull fresco is one
of several at Knossos.

Throne Room, Knossos
The great palace was built
between 1700 and 1400
BCE. Its so-called Throne
Room has wall paintings
featuring griffins. The
griffins may have been a
symbol of divinity or a
heraldic motif. The basin
was probably filled with
water, perhaps for ritual
washing or even used as
an aquarium.

OPPOSITE:
Lasithi Plateau and Dikti Mountains
This windy plateau has been inhabited since at least 6000 BCE, thanks to its fertile soil caused by alluvial run-off from melting snow on the Dikti Mountains. These peaks, said to have been the birthplace of Zeus, rise to 2,148m (7,047ft).

ABOVE:
Holy Trinity Church, Agia Roumeli
Accessible only by foot or boat, the small village of Agia Roumeli lies between the wild mountains of southwestern Crete and the Libyan Sea. A walk in the direction of the Samaria Gorge leads to this whitewashed Byzantine church.

Matala Beach

The many caves in the cliffs at Matala were dug from Neolithic times. Judging by their size, they were probably used as dwellings. In the 1960s, the caves were occupied by hippies from around the world. Canadian folk singer Joni Mitchell wrote her 1971 song 'Carey' about her time with the Matala hippies, with 'filthy fingernails' and 'beach tar' on her feet.

LEFT:

Church of St John, Lentas

The small Byzantine Church of St John was built in the 14th century, close to a ruined sanctuary to the god of medicine Asclepius, first established in the 4th century BCE.

OPPOSITE:

Samariá Gorge

A popular destination for hikers, this dramatic gorge is 16km (10 miles) long. In the section known as 'The Gates', the rock walls, only 4m (13ft) apart, soar to a height of almost 300m (980ft). The pale rocks are largely limestone, dolomite and marble, giving rise to the name for the surrounding mountains: Lefka Ori ('White Mountains').

ALL PHOTOGRAPHS:

Villa with a Sea View
Since the 1970s, tourism has dramatically overtaken agriculture as Crete's key source of income. Today the island has three airports receiving international flights: Heraklion, Chana and Sitia. Accommodation ranges from campsites to high-end villas and hotels, with Crete offering more than 30 per cent of the whole country's 5-star beds.

ALL PHOTOGRAPHS:
**Olive Groves,
Fruit and Oil**
It is believed that a handful of Crete's olive trees date back many centuries – possibly millennia – based on the width of their trunks, which sometimes reach over 10m (32ft). Many of the trees on Crete bear *elitses*, meaning 'tiny olives'. Despite their diminutive size, this variety is the source of some of the world's best olive oil. When still green, a few are harvested as table olives, but the majority are left till black and ripe. Today, olives are harvested using battery-powered sticks, which beat them from the branches. Sacks of olives are taken to the olive press, where leaves are removed and they are rinsed. The olives are then cold pressed, releasing the oil.

Arkadi Monastery
Probably founded by a
monk named Arkadios,
this monastery was
established by the 14th
century. Its 16th-century
Renaissance church shows
both ornate Baroque
and elegant Roman
influences, signposting
its development under
Venetian rule.

Agia Triada Monastery
Dedicated to the Holy
Trinity, this 17th-century
monastery was built
in pink stone by two
monk brothers from
the powerful Venetian
Zangaroli family. It
was Ieremias Zangaroli
himself who designed the
monastery, influenced by
the great 16th-century
Italian Mannerist architect
Sebastiano Serlio.

FAR LEFT:
Rethymno
Today, Rethymno's Venetian harbour is lined with fish tavernas and cafés. This is the place to try local specialities, including *chochlioi boubouristi* (fried snails), *kaltsounia* (cheese pies) and lamb with *stamnagathi*, a local green.

TOP AND BOTTOM LEFT:
Seafood
In Crete, the catch of the day in coastal villages and towns can include inexpensive sardines (bottom left), anchovies, smelt and squid, which are usually served grilled lightly in olive oil, or the pricier octopus (often eaten as a *mezze*), cuttlefish (stewed in tomato sauce) and lobster (fashionably served with macaroni).

Aegean Islands

The ancient Greek name for the Aegean Sea was *Archipelago*, meaning 'chief sea'. Since this sea is remarkable for its hundreds of islands, the name came to mean, first, the islands themselves, then any island group. In addition to Crete, from south to north the main island groups are the Dodecanese, in the southeast, including Rhodes and Kos; the Saronic Islands, close to the mainland and administered as part of Attica; the Cyclades, with the largest islands, Naxos and Andros; the Sporades, along Greece's east coast, including Skiathos and Skopelos; and the North Aegean, including Chios and Lesbos.

The Cyclades are the biggest island group, comprising about 220 islands. The name of the group refers to the islands 'around' (*cyclic*) the ancient religious sanctuary on the island of Delos. On most islands, the main town or village is known only as Chora, simply meaning 'town'. To the east, in the Dodecanese, tourists are drawn to busy Rhodes, offering a history rich with ambitious merchants and Crusader knights.

OPPOSITE:

Church of Panagia Paraportiani, Chora, Mykonos
The name of this church means 'Our Lady of the Side Gate', as it was built at the side entrance to the Byzantine and Venetian *kastro*, or fortification, in today's Kastro neighbourhood. It is not one church, but an organic colony of five chapels.

Cape Falakro, Lemnos
According to myth, Lemnos was the site of the forge of Hephaestus, god of fire and blacksmiths. In the Miocene period, this region saw intensive volcanic activity, resulting in strangely shaped rock formations where lava made sudden contact with seawater. *Falakro* means 'bald', referring to the bald head-like orbs seen here.

ABOVE AND OPPOSITE:

Dovecotes of Tarambados, Tinos

Less visited than most of the Cyclades, Tinos only becomes busy around 15 August, during the pilgrimage to the icon of the Virgin in the Church of Panagia Evangelistria. The island is known for its many dovecotes, introduced by the Venetians in the 15th century.

The two-storey stone dovecotes are decorated with schist tiles arranged in geometric patterns, flowers, trees and suns (see opposite). Villagers believe the designs attract the pigeons, which are kept for their meat and manure. The lower floors of the dovecotes are used for storing tools.

ALL PHOTOGRAPHS:
Petaloudes Valley, Rhodes

Every year, after the spring wet season, the 'Valley of the Butterflies' is home to thousands of *Euplagia quadripunctaria rhodosensis*, the Rhodes subspecies of the Jersey tiger moth. The valley's Oriental sweetgum trees give off a scent that attracts the day-flying moths, while the high humidity allows them to aestivate, or enter a state of dormancy, to shelter from the summer heat.

OPPOSITE:
Lalaria, Skiathos

The pebble beach and wave-worn rock arch of Lalaria are reached only by boat, of which there are many leaving Skiathos's old port. When the northern *meltemi* wind is high, which it frequently is during July and August, it may be too squally for small boats to make the journey.

ABOVE:
Tourlitis Lighthouse, Andros

The first lighthouse on this rocky islet, just off the coast of Andros Town, was built in 1897. It was destroyed during World War II, but rebuilt in 1994 by the local Goulandris oil family, in memory of their daughter Violanda. Its fully automated light can be seen for 20 nautical kilometres (11 nautical miles).

OPPOSITE:

Pyrgi, Chios

Pyrgi is known as the 'Painted Village' because of the black and white motifs on the facades of its houses. This is the traditional seat of the Mastic Villages, where mastic tree resin is harvested for use in chewing gum and desserts.

TOP LEFT:

Making *Kataifi*

Shredded filo pastry is formed on a spinning hotplate. The hair-like result is wrapped around nuts and spices, then baked and drizzled in syrup to make sweet *kataifi* desserts.

BOTTOM FAR LEFT:

Preparing Pasta, Lesbos

There are dozens of regional Greek pastas, often made with wheat, sheep or goat's milk, olive oil and eggs. One method is to rub the dough between the fingers then leave it to dry in the sun.

BOTTOM NEAR LEFT:

Cheese, Agios Efstratios

This tiny, sparsely populated island lives by fishing, bee-keeping and cheese-making with sheep and goat's milk. Here the drained curds are being pressed into moulds.

OPPOSITE:

Church of Panagia, Chora, Folegandros

Folegandros's largest settlement, Chora, was built on the cusp of a 200m (650ft) high cliff. The whitewashed homes of its *kastro* are packed closely together for protection. A 15-minute walk from the village, up a zigzagging path, is the Church of Panagia.

RIGHT:

Folegandros

Folegandros makes its living from fishing and agriculture, although fresh water and cultivatable land are rare in this dry, rocky place. Today, the additional income from tourists looking for peace and quiet has prevented communities from having to seek work on the mainland.

Milos

The southwesternmost island in the Cyclades is volcanic in origin, with soft, easily
eroded tuff among its rocks. Caves, stacks, arches and blowholes are common along
Milos' rugged coast. The island was an important commercial centre in antiquity.
It was here the so-called *Venus de Milo* statue
was found, depicting Aphrodite,
the goddess of love.

ABOVE:

Aging *Arsenico Kefalotyri*, Filoti, Naxos

In the mountains of central Naxos, cheese is left to age in *mitata*, shepherds' huts built from locally gathered stones without mortar. Chief among the cheeses of Filoti is *arsenico kefalotyri*, produced from sheep or goat's milk and whey. Although sweet at first, it becomes spicy after maturing for a few weeks.

OPPOSITE:

Museum of Samian Wine, Vathy, Samos

This museum is housed in an old winery, where giant wooden barrels still stand. Visitors can also admire manual presses, pumps and filters, as well as the tools used by coopers to make the wooden casks. On Samos, the Muscat grape is widely grown, producing typically sweet, golden wines such as Nectar and Samos Doux.

Windmills, Chora, Mykonos

A landmark in the town of Chora, and a symbol of the Cyclades, five windmills stand on a windy hill overlooking the restaurants and cafés of 'Little Venice'. Many windmills were built on Mykonos by the Venetians in the 16th century, but their construction continued until the early 20th century. They were mainly used to mill wheat.

OPPOSITE:

Klima, Milos

In the fishing village of Klima, the colourfully painted houses were carved into the rocks of the cliff, their doors just an arm's length from the breaking waves on the narrow pebbly beach. On the ground floor of each house is a *syrmata*, or boat garage.

LEFT:

Katapola, Amorgos

In the harbour of the main port of Amorgos, numerous traditional wooden fishing boats, known as *kaikis*, are moored. These boats are made using methods similar to those practised 5,000 years ago, often using pine. Each is painted vividly to the fisherman's own taste.

ABOVE AND OPPOSITE:

Oia, Santorini

A prominent characteristic of Cycladic architecture is whitewashed, cube-like buildings, built close together to offer protection from the elements. In Santorini's Oia, structures gain purchase by being carved into the cliff itself. Churches are topped with bright blue domes and simple, smoothly sculpted belltowers (*see above*).

The town of Oia (*see opposite*) clings to the steep slope of the caldera lip that forms the island of Santorini. Santorini is the largest island of a small, circular archipelago. It is the result of repeated cycles of shield volcano construction and caldera collapse. A devastating eruption 3,600 years ago may have resulted in the decline of the Minoan civilization on Crete to the south.

OPPOSITE:

Syrtos, Skopelos

There are thousands of Greek dances from all the islands and regions. Dances are performed during festivals and at weddings and other celebrations. In the popular Syrtos, dancers link hands, following a leader who periodically breaks away to perform improvized steps.

RIGHT:

Cretan Lyra and Laouto

The Cretan lyra (*left*), played with a bow, is central to the traditional music of the Aegean Islands. Plucked with a long plectrum, the laouto's long neck gives it a high string tension and a bright tone. It is often played as accompaniment to the lyra.

OPPOSITE:
Palace of the Grand Master of the Knights of Rhodes
Parts of the current palace were built by the Byzantines in the 7th century. In the 14th century, the Crusading Knights Hospitaller occupied Rhodes and greatly modified the existing structure. From this base, they fought against Barbary pirates and the Ottomans across the Mediterranean.

ABOVE:
House of Cleopatra, Delos
At the centre of the Cyclades, little Delos was said to be the birthplace of Apollo and Artemis. From 900 BCE, it became a cultural centre and major trading port. This ruined villa boasts a pair of headless statues of its owners, a wealthy Athenian couple called Cleopatra and Dioscurides.

207

OPPOSITE:

Agia Theodoti, Ios

Away from Ios's hectic steep-laned Chora, known for its party scene, hikers in Ios's unspoiled hilly interior are likely to meet no one except the occasional farmer and hear little except the ringing of goat bells. All but around 300 of Ios's inhabitants live in Chora.

ABOVE:

Chora, Folegandros

A speciality in the tavernas of Chora is *ntakos*, a rusk topped with tomatoes, feta, capers and olives. Perfect for washing it down, particularly in winter, is *rakomelo*, made with *raki* or *tsipouro* grape pomace brandy mixed with honey and spices, such as cinnamon or cardamom.

LEFT:

***Panagia Gorgona,
Kini, Syros***
'Virgin Mary the
Mermaid', patroness of
fishermen, is a memorial
to local fishermen lost at
sea. This centrepiece of a
fountain on the seafront
at Kini was created
by Athenian sculptor
Giorgos Xenoulis.

OPPOSITE:

Ermoupoli, Syros
Ermoupoli was not
founded until the 1820s,
during the Greek War
of Independence, when
Syros' neutrality led
to its becoming home
to countless refugees.
Ermoupoli grew to be
a major port and ship-
building centre. Built
in 1848, the yellow St
Nicholas's Church is
crowned by a bright
blue dome.

LEFT:

Marble, Thassos

Thassos is the northernmost significant Aegean Island, just 7km (4 miles) south of the Macedonian mainland. The island is formed largely of metamorphic rocks: gneiss, schist and – most valuably – marble. Thassos marble is famed for its translucent quality.

OPPOSITE:

Marble Quarry, Thassos

By the 6th century BCE, Thassos marble was being exported to the mainland and the coast of Asia Minor. During the Archaic period, numerous *kouros* statues of idealized young men were carved from Thassos marble. Later, the Romans shipped large quantities of pure-white marble for use back home.

OPPOSITE:
Pothia, Kalymnos
Kalymnos is known for being one of the wealthiest Greek islands, despite the fact that less than one-fifth of its land is cultivatable. In the past, free-diving for sponges was a major source of wealth, while the island's female inhabitants built a vibrant industry around exquisitely hand-painted headscarfs.

ABOVE:
Climbing in Grande Grotta, Kalymnos
Today, Kalymnos is a global rock-climbing destination, thanks to its mild climate and nearly 2,000 mapped and bolted routes among its limestone cliffs, caves and boulders. The popular Grande Grotta cave routes offer views over to Telendos Island, which has a population of under 100.

Drying Octopus, Santorini

To make octopus tender enough to grill, it must be dried in the sun for at least a day. This not only eliminates any remaining water, but the seasalt preserves and seasons the flesh. On the islands, octopus is often eaten as a *meze*, seasoned with lemon and grilled over charcoal.

Olympos, Karpathos

Home to around 500 people, the ridge-top village of Olympos in northern Karpathos is a window back in time, due to its long isolation from the outside world. The precipitous, switchbacking road to the village from Pigadia, the island's main village and port, was asphalted only in the 1980s. Before then, the only way here was boat or donkey.

RIGHT:

Olympos, Karpathos

A unique local dialect is spoken in Olympos, and some of the village's older women still wear traditional dress – a black apron and headscarf.

OPPOSITE TOP LEFT:

Baking Bread, Olympos

For Easter and other festivals, bread is baked in an outdoor communal brick oven. The appointed baker rotates and removes loaves using a giant spatula-like tool.

OPPOSITE TOP RIGHT:

St Minas Festival, Olympos

There are vestiges of a matriarchy in Olympos, a village where women are not only the main keepers of tradition but are also central to the restaurants and other businesses that are now sustaining this community.

OPPOSITE BOTTOM LEFT:

Pera Panagia Festival, Olympos

During festivals, the women of Olympos wear brightly coloured traditional dresses and headscarfs with necklaces of golden coins.

OPPOSITE BOTTOM RIGHT:

Decorated Easter Bread

For Easter, sweet breads shaped into snakes are decorated with dyed eggs, called *avgoules*.

ALL PHOTOGRAPHS:
Roadside Shrines
Roadside shrines, known as *proskinitari*, are sometimes erected by family members where a loved-one has died in a road accident. They often resemble miniature churches. Sadly, they can be seen by roadsides all over the islands, from Kos (opposite) and Leros (right) in the south to Thassos in the north (above).